Why are We Deaf
to the Cry of the Earth?

SEAN McDONAGH

VERITAS

Published 2001 by
Veritas Publications
7/8 Lower Abbey Street
Dublin 1
Ireland

Email: publications@veritas.ie
Website: www.veritas.ie

ISBN 185390 544 5

A catalogue for this book is available from the British Library.

Veritas books are printed on paper made from the wood pulp of managed forests. For every tree felled, at least one tree is planted, thereby renewing natural resources.

Design by Pierce Design
Printed by Betaprint Ltd

Contents

Why are we deaf to the Cry of the Earth?

In our modern educational setting students learn mainly through rational processes, especially analytical methods. In traditional societies they learned through stories. Jesus didn't define or analyse love, He told the story of the 'Good Samaritan'.

The following story highlights the inability of many people, especially those in leadership roles in institutions, to deal adequately with the widening gap between the rich and the poor and the rampant destruction of the environment in an effective and systematic way.

> A group of people were invited to a banquet in a beautiful medieval castle situated in a beautiful courtyard. It was a splendid feast with a profusion of sumptuous dishes, a delicious range of wines and other drinks, superb service and an excellent orchestra to entertain the guests as they ate. The food was so good and the drinks so delicious that the guests simply couldn't get enough. They continued to gorge themselves long after the point of satiation.
>
> As the night wore on, instead of ending the meal, relaxing and going home, the revellers became more and more intent on securing additional helpings of the mouth-watering food. Their demands became so

voracious that all the food was consumed. The master of the house, in order to avoid embarrassment, sent out his servants, backed by the militia, to collect more food from the poor inhabitants in the surrounding countryside.

Fuel to cook the food also ran out. The cooks ordered some servants to begin chopping away at the timber pillars that supported the roof in order to get firewood to continue cooking. After a while some of the wooden pillars began to sag a little and cracks appeared in the ceiling. But the servants and banqueters were so absorbed in the meal that they were completely unaware of the long-term consequence of their actions. They had no time to consider that, unless they stopped hacking at the supporting pillars, the ceiling would eventually come crashing down on their heads.

The din, buzz and activity in the kitchen and dining hall were electrifying. People were milling around the cooking stoves, shouting orders for more food and eating with relish. Yet not everyone was caught up in the frenzy. A small number of people stood by the door with neither plates nor glasses in their hands. They carried placards denouncing the diners, pointing out that the heavy cost of the meal was been borne by poor, starving peasants in the surrounding countryside. Others with an eye to the environmental consequences, aware that the beams were sagging and that a tragedy was imminent, implored the diners to end the meal and thus avert the disaster.

A few of those eating would occasionally stop to listen to their heartfelt pleas: they might even cast a fleeting glance towards the ceiling. But as soon as a waiter with more food came close they would lose interest and join in the scramble for more. The majority of those who were celebrating, however, didn't take any notice at all. They were simply so engrossed in the meal that nothing else really mattered.[1]

Many parts of Ireland are renowned for their beauty. Places like Killarney, the Burren and Donegal spring to mind as areas well patronised by tourists. North Tipperary, where I grew up in the 1950s and 1960s, does not figure prominently on the tourist trail. And yet it is a place of great beauty, with rivers, mountains, and especially Lough Derg, as part of our heritage. Growing up before the advent of television meant that the world of nature was a source of joy and pleasure.

Like the Jesuit poet Gerard Manley Hopkins in 'Pied Beauty' I can say 'Glory be to God for dappled things...'.

When I came to know these places in my teens I had very little sense of foreboding that humankind were wreaking havoc on the world of nature. The thoughtless, destructive approach to nature is captured vividly by Hopkins again in his poem 'Binsey Poplars' which he wrote after revisiting a destroyed river bank that he knew so well.

> O if we but knew what we do
> When we delve or hew-
> Hack and rack the growing green!
> Since country is so tender
> To touch her being so slender,
> That, like this sleek and seeing ball
> But a prick will make no eye at all,
> We we, even where we mean
> To mend her we end her,
> When we hue and delve;
> After-comers cannot guess the beauty been...

The damage today is not merely to a single riverbank. During my 20 years as a missionary in the Philippines I witnessed enormous destruction to the rainforest, mangrove forests and coral reefs. But the problem is truly global. A city like Manila is choking with air pollution and smog. It and many other Third World cities face massive problems supplying basic services like water and sanitation to its burgeoning population during this decade.

However, environmental damage is not confined to Third World countries. It is truly a global phenomenon and must be tackled as such by every human being and every human institution. During my time in the Philippines I became involved in environmental issues. I worked with groups that were trying to protect and replant rainforests and also with the anti-nuclear non-government organisations. I also began to encourage the Churches, particularly the Catholic Church, to become more pro-active in environmental matters, through talks, articles and by helping to draft the first pastoral letter exclusively devoted to environmental issues – *What is Happening to Our Beautiful Land?* – which appeared in 1988.

As we begin this new millennium, everyone must face the fact that our modern industrial society has taken a huge toll on the fabric of life on earth during the past 100 years. The various industrial revolutions over the past two centuries, from steam to microchip and biotech, have delivered enormous benefits to about one-fifth of humanity. This group includes the majority of people in First World countries and the elite in the Third World. Many of us live longer, are better fed and housed than any previous generation. We have access to choices, especially in the area of technology and medicine, that even kings couldn't dream of in the past.

But there is a dark side to these developments that needs to be addressed. Put briefly, my thesis is as follows. We are destroying our air, water and the life-giving quality of sunlight. We are poisoning our soils and causing the extinction of a vast number of the creatures that God has placed on this earth with us. Every part of the globe and every ecosystem has been affected. The damage everywhere is grave. In some situations, like the extinction of species, it is irreversible. Unfortunately, Church leaders of all traditions, in common with their counterparts in the educational, industrial, political

and financial establishments, have been slow to understand the
magnitude of the destruction and the urgency with which we
must halt environmental degradation and, where possible, heal
the earth.

Destroying the Earth

My main thesis is that humans are causing changes of a
biological and geological order of magnitude. We are ending
the Cenozoic period.

Much of the data regarding the deteriorating state of our air,
water, soils and tropical forests is now generally accepted by
the scientific community. In November 1992 over 1,500
scientists, including many Nobel prize-winners, issued a wake-
up call. They stated that human beings and the natural world
were on a collision course. No more than one or a few decades
remain before the chance to avoid the threats we now confront
will be lost.

All that is possible in this pamphlet is to look at a number
of global and national environmental challenges and to
discern how Christians might respond to environmental
destruction from the well-spring of their own religious
tradition.

I call on two voices to set the stage for my presentation. The
first is that of Klaus Topfer, executive director of the United
Nations Environment Programme. His report stated that the
'main threats to human survival were posed by water
shortages, global warming and a new danger – worldwide
nitrogen pollution.'[2]

The second came from Pope John Paul II on January 17th,
2001. The pope called for what he called an 'ecological

conversion'. The Pope stated that 'if we scan the regions of our planet, we immediately see that humanity has disappointed God's expectations. Man, especially in our time, has without hesitation devastated wooded plains and valleys, polluted waters, disfigured the earth's habitat, made the air unbreathable, disturbed the hydrogeological and atmospheric spheres and turned luxuriant areas into deserts and undertaken forms of unrestrained industrialisation, humiliating the flower-garden of the universe to use the image of Dante Alighieri' (Paradiso, XX11, 151). We must therefore encourage and support the 'ecological conversion' that in recent decades has made humanity more sensitive to the catastrophe to which it has been heading. Man is no longer the Creator's 'steward', but an autonomous despot, who is finally beginning to understand that he must stop at the edge of the abyss.[3]

Land

Poor land management, overgrazing, chemical agriculture, monocropping, deforestation and human population pressures have caused soil erosion and desertification on an unprecedented scale.[4]

About 3,500 million hectares, an area the size of North and South America, are affected by desertification. Each year at least another six million hectares are irretrievably lost to desertification, and a further 21 million hectares are so degraded that crop production is severely affected. Professor David Pimentel and his team at Cornell University in Ithaca, New York, estimates that, world-wide, about 85 billion tonnes of soil are lost each year. Most of this damage, unfortunately, is in the Third World, where between 30 and 40 tonnes per hectare are eroded each year. Even in the US 17 tonnes of topsoil per hectare are eroded with each cropping.[5] Top soil is precious; without it no crops will grow and pasture land will not be fertile. No machine can readily create topsoil. It builds up slowly and takes between 200 and 1,000 years for 2.5 cm of topsoil to build up.

Land degradation is also found in Europe. Desertification is normally associated with Africa, but it is also a factor in Europe, where it now threatens 12 per cent of its land area. Intensive agriculture on marginal lands, grazing unsuitable pastures, forest fires, urban sprawl and tourism have all taken their toll on the land, especially in a country like Spain.[6]

During the past three decades, overgrazing by sheep, facilitated by the EU-funded Sheep Headage payment and the Irish government's ewe premium payments, has led to enormous levels of soil erosion on the hills and mountains on the west coast of Ireland. The schemes were designed to help farmers in poorer areas, but an increase in the number of sheep in the country from 3.3 million in 1980 to 8.9 million in 1991 took a terrible toll on heather moorlands. The Irish Peatland Conservation Council estimates that 50 peatlands of conservation value throughout the Republic have been extensively damaged. These cover over 54,220 hectares.[7]

Genetically Engineered Foods

In recent years many people have become worried by developments in genetics and biotechnology that allow genes to be moved between various species that would never interact through normal breeding processes. Today, plants and animals with genes taken from completely unrelated species are being engineered in the laboratories of biotechnology companies and released into the environment. Many people, including eminent scientists like Dr Arpad Puszai, are worried about the effects of such genetically engineered organisms on human health and on the wider environment. To date, very scant resources have been made available by governments to 'study the health, nutritional or environmental consequence of gene manipulation'. The US lawyer Steven Druker alleged at a Biotech conference in Edinburgh in February 2000 that there has been a cover-up in the US Food and Drug Administration (FDA). The FDA introduced a standard of proof known as 'substantive equivalence'. This assumes that the GE food is substantially equivalent to non-GE foods. Druker maintains that some FDA scientists had doubts about this policy and communicated these to the senior management in the FDA. They refused to act and allowed powerful transnational corporations to sell GE foods in the US. The proponents of genetically engineered crops say that they are promoting biotechnology in order to increase food production, especially for the poor in Third World countries. Many people are sceptical about their motivation and feel that it is driven by a desire for increased profits rather than from any altruistic intent. As the Prince of Wales said in his Reith lecture in May 2000, 'If a fraction of the money currently being invested in developing genetically manipulated crops were applied to understanding and improving traditional systems of agriculture, which have stood the all-important test of time, the results would be remarkable.'[8]

In September 2000 the US Food and Drug Administration began a safety investigation when it became clear that a variety of genetically engineered corn that was banned for human consumption was found in a popular snack. The GE corn is called Starlink. It is produced by Aventis Corporation and contains an inbuilt pesticide that could cause allergic reactions in some people. The traces of the banned protein were found in cornmeal taco shells by Friends of the Earth. These taco shells were being distributed by Kraft, which is a subsidiary of the cigarette company Philip Morris.[9]

Even those who accept that a particular genetically engineered crop will not damage human health or the environment are worried about the scramble to patent seeds, animals and living organisms which has gathered speed in recent years. They believe that over a short period of time patenting will remove many life forms from the public commons where they have served humans and other creatures for millennia. Under a patenting regime these life forms will become the property of northern transnational corporations. Life will only have value in so far as it generates a profitable return on investment for large companies who in a decade or so could control the seed banks for many of the staple foods of the world. The possibility that a small number of multinational companies will control the seeds of the world's staple crops is truly frightening.

The food security of Third World countries could very easily be compromised if farmers have to buy patented seeds each year from agribusiness companies. Even in countries like Canada, agribusiness companies like Monsanto have taken lawsuits against farmers who they allege are planting patented seeds and not buying them from the company. Monsanto have engaged the services of an investigative agency to gather information on over 1000 farmers whom they consider are cheating on patented seeds.[10] The affected farmers have coined a new word, 'bio-serfs', to capture the feudal relationship which now exists between many seed companies and farmers. It is little wonder that across the world patenting seeds and animals is now seen as a major economic, development and ethical issue.

In 1998, before the European Parliament voted on the life-patenting directive entitled the EU Directive on the Patenting of Biological Inventions, environmental organisations in Ireland, especially VOICE, attempted to ignite a public debate on the issue. Despite the explicit teaching of the Bible that life is a gift from God and that there are limits to human control over life, the Churches in Ireland were silent on this issue. It would appear that the pro-life stance is very selective indeed.

Water

Human activity is polluting water in the oceans, rivers, aquifers and lakes. In mid-February 2000 a cyanide spill from a gold mine in Northern Romania entered the river Tisza, a tributary of the Danube, destroying aquatic life for hundreds of miles down stream.[11] Pollution is also a problem in Asia. The Indus, one of the great rivers of Asia, is heavily polluted.

More than 97 per cent of all the water on Earth is sea water. During the UNESCO proclaimed International Year of the Ocean in 1998 it emerged that the oceans are being over-fished and polluted at an unprecedented rate. Important areas of the oceans close to the continental shelf are contaminated with human, agricultural, industrial and radioactive waste. Much of this is toxic and carcinogenic. Because we have tended to treat the oceans as sewers the Baltic, Mediterranean, Black, Caspian, Bering, Yellow and South China Seas have all been seriously damaged in recent decades. The water of the Black Sea, once a flourishing eco-system, is now considered to be 90 per cent dead. The Aral Sea has diminished by one-third and what remains is heavily polluted. Wind storms blow the toxic sand from the exposed seabed on to villages, contaminating crops and exposing humans and animals to the poison.

Depleting the Oceans

On another front over-fishing is depleting the oceans and leaving them barren. Many people feel that the oceans are so vast and the variety of fish so abundant that there would always be vast quantities of fish in the sea. We are now learning how false those assumptions are. According to a report by the UN Food and Agricultural Organisation (FAO) in 1995 over 70 per cent of the world's marine fish stocks are either 'fully-to-heavily exploited', overexploited, or slowly recovering.[12]

Only one per cent of the fresh water of the world is available for human use in either agriculture, industry or for domestic purposes. Access to this water is very inequitable. World-wide, the demand for water is doubling every 21 years. Supply cannot keep pace with demand as populations soar and cities

explode. Access to clean water is also not equitable. While rich
people around the world can afford the luxury of fresh-water
swimming pools, poor women in the Third World have to walk
miles to fetch water for their basic family needs.

Today the water situation in the Middle East and North
Africa is precarious. North-eastern China, Western and
Southern India, Pakistan, much of South America and
countries in Central America like Mexico face water scarcity.
Somewhere in the region of 260 rivers flow through two
countries or more. Only a handful of these countries have
signed treaties regulating their respective access to the water.[13]
As a result, competition between adjacent countries for access
to water resources is causing friction and could lead to outright
hostilities in the future. For example, Egypt and Ethiopia seem
to be on a collision course over access to the waters of the Nile.
The river originates in Ethiopia. Until recently the Ethiopians
used only a small fraction of the river's water. They are now
building small dams. The Egyptians fear that this will affect the
water supply to their farmers. Unequal access to the waters of
the Jordan Rivers are fuelling Palestinian resentment on the
West Bank.

Water in Ireland

Anyone who lives here knows that Ireland is blessed with a
plentiful supply of rain. While the level of pollution in Ireland
has not reached the level that it has in Eastern Europe there is
no room for complacency. An editorial in the *Irish Times* (14
March 2000) stated that 'Ireland's rivers have gone, in little
more than a generation, from being almost pristine pure and
clear to overblown imitations of open sewers and chemical
drains.' The editorial was in response to a report published by
the 'Three Rivers Project' which chronicles the decline in water
quality in the Liffey, the Boyne and the Suir.

It is now accepted even by the EPA that the quality of water
in many Irish rivers and lakes has deteriorated in recent

decades.[14] Fish kills, unfortunately, still happen each summer. This is normally due to the increased levels of phosphorus entering our rivers from a variety of sources, including sewage treatment plants, factories and farms. The subsequent algal bloom depletes the supply of oxygen and causes the fish to die.

The Greenhouse Effect

Between the middle of 1998 and October 2000 oil prices jumped from $10 to $35 a barrel. In Britain protesters against the high price of fuel blockaded oil terminals and brought the country to a standstill. The protesters demanded that the government cut excise duty on petrol in order to reduce the price to the consumer and haulage companies. When the chancellor, Gordon Brown, with the backing of the Prime Minister refused to cut taxes, Labour's rating in polls dropped precipitously. In a Lazarus-like turn around, the no-hoper Conservatives looked like they might win an election. The truckers' action in Ireland on 15 September 2000 also called for a reduction in excise duty on diesel. Their message was clear: consumers want cheap petrol no matter what the consequences.

Unfortunately there was little strong, forceful leadership from politicians. Few were willing to mention the two words – environment or greenhouse effect – during the second week of September. The atmospheric concentration of carbon dioxide, methane, chloroflourocarbons (CFCs) and other 'greenhouse' gases are expected to increase by 30 per cent during the next 50 years. This build-up is likely to increase the Earth's surface temperature by between 1.5 and 4.5 degrees centigrade by the year 2030. This will cause major, and in the main, deleterious climatic changes. In Northern latitudes, winters will probably be shorter and wetter, summers longer and drier. Sub-tropical areas might become drier and more arid and tropical ones wetter. The changes will have major, but as yet unpredictable effects on agriculture and natural eco-systems.

As the oceans warm up and expand, sea levels will rise, leading to severe flooding over lowland areas. Unfortunately, the poorest countries, which emit very little greenhouse gases, will suffer most from climate change. Much of Bangladesh and the low-lying areas in many countries will simply disappear and create migration problems. According to *Time* (4 September 2000), 'In Alaska melting permafrost has produced "roller coaster" roads, power lines tilted at crazy angles and houses sinking up to their window sashes as the ground liquefies.'[15]

Storms of great ferocity, like hurricane Mitch that slammed into Central America in October 1998, the devastating floods and mudslides that killed over 10,000 on the Caribbean coast of Venezuela, and the devastating wind storms that battered France after Christmas 1999 will probably become more frequent. As Dr Mike Hulme of the University of East Anglia, Norwich, puts it: 'We are running massive risks by altering the climate of our planet in ways we do not fully understand let alone are able to predict with confidence. ...And the longer we continue to rely on a carbon-based energy economy, the greater the risks will be.'[16] Recent studies predict that the global warming will not benefit Ireland and other countries in Northern Europe. An increase in temperature in the Arctic could interfere with the Gulf Stream and thus we could see a significant drop in temperature in Ireland, Britain and Norway.[17]

In the run up to the United Nations meeting on climate change in Kyoto, Japan, in December 1997, a group of almost 2000 scientists that comprise the Intergovernmental Panel on Climate Change (IPCC) called for a 60 per cent reduction in the use of fossil fuel. Unfortunately, the politicians, who attended the meeting, representing 160 countries, could only agree to a miserly 5.2% below 1990 levels by the year 2010. Even so, many countries, particularly the US, have made little progress towards implementing the treaty. In fact the US Senate has not even ratified the treaty.

Until November 2000 the Irish Government had not faced up to this global challenge even though climate change will cause huge suffering for poor people. Ireland committed itself to limiting greenhouse gas emissions to 13 per cent above 1990 levels by the year 2008-10. A report published by the Environmental Protection Agency in August 2000 entitled *Emissions of Atmospheric Pollutants in Ireland 1990-1998* claims that the greenhouse gas emissions for 1998 exceeded the limits agreed for the year 2010 under the Kyoto Protocol. According to Mr Michael McGettigan, a co-author of the report, 'Ireland faces the censure of other signatories to the Kyoto Protocol and a possible restriction on goods manufactured using processes that do not conform to the reduced-emissions policy.'[18] Greenhouse gas emission in Ireland rose by 18 per cent between 1990 and 1998. The annual growth rate now is over 4 per cent.[19] Ireland may exceed its greenhouse gas target by a massive 180 per cent according to a front page story in the *Irish Independent* on 18 September 2000.

The Irish government needs to invest in and promote wind, water and wave power in order to move away from our over-dependence. A levy on fossil fuel similar to the one being introduced by the Labour Government in Britain is urgently needed. This levy is not draconian and will only add 0.45p per unit to business energy bills. The levy will collect £1.1 billion per annum and this will be returned to industry through reductions that employers pay in National Insurance contribution for their employees.[20] The possibility of such a tax was contained in a Green Paper on energy published by the Department of Public Enterprise in September 1999.

On 2 November 2000 the Irish Government published a comprehensive plan to tackle Ireland's growing 'greenhouse' gas emissions in preparation for the meeting on global warming in the Hague. Among the initiatives mentioned were: unspecified tax on fossil fuel; closure or conversion of the

Moneypoint coal-fired power station; reducing the national herd to curb methane emissions; an option for industry to engage in carbon trading; encouragement to new house-holders to build more energy-efficient houses and tax support for more fuel-efficient cars.

Will the plan work? I am not too sure. Unless the goals are much more specific and the methodology and agents to implement the plan are stated much more clearly I would have my doubts. Voluntary efforts from industry in other areas, for example, waste management have proved ineffective. We still do not have a tax on plastic bags! There is no reason to think that it will be any different with energy consumption.

Frank McDonald, the environment correspondent of the *Irish Times*, points out that there are a number of very significant loopholes in the Minister's plan. Manufacturing one tonne of cement releases one tonne of carbon dioxide into the atmosphere. Nevertheless, these emission do not count in processing an application to build a cement factory.[21] Finally, it will be very difficult to break the love affair that Irish people have with their car without a massive education programme and real support for alternative transport and energy initiatives. The document just does not address this in any competent and creative way.

It is very difficult to see Ireland doing anything significant about tackling global warming unless there is a willingness to do a greenhouse audit on the £40 billion National Development Plan. The present plan with its emphasis on a massive road building programme will only exacerbate an already terrible record in greenhouse gas emissions. At a time of unprecedented affluence we should be putting most emphasis on public transport. Priority should be given to making rail travel more attractive and accessible. Calls for car-free days for cities or towns without good public transport and proper facilities for pedestrians and cyclists are hypocritical.[22]

A former speaker of the House of Representatives in the US, Tip O'Neill, is reported to have said that all politics is local. Whatever about politics, all environments are local. I am going to look at three local environments: the Burren in north Clare, Lough Derg which touches Clare, Tipperary and Galway, and the recent building programme in the west Clare seaside town of Kilkee.

The Burren

Today I still find great joy in nature, especially in the Burren in County Clare. This area of Ireland, comprising about 150 square miles in north Clare and south Galway, has so many wonderful gifts. The sun shining on the limestone that was sculptured by a receding ice-sheet during the last ice age is a joy to behold. The mood on a wet day, with overcast, leaden skies mingling with the grey of the limestone, has its own appeal. At first sight the rocks seem barren, but a profusion of life lives in the clints and grykes that have been weathered by rain water for aeons. On the hills one finds a diversity of plants, including spring gentians, mountain avens, burnet roses, carline thistles, heather, harebells, O'Kelly's spotted-orchids, from regions as far apart as the Arctic and the Mediterranean. 28 of the 30 species of butterflies that are native to Ireland can be found in the Burren.

Mountains like Mullaghmore have a magical quality about them. Many of the 'green roads' offer spectacular views. I particularly like walking on a summer's day on the one in the north Burren above Black Head. The Burren with its profusion of flowering plants rises above on the right, with maybe a kestrel hovering around looking for its next meal, while the blue waters of Galway Bay and the Connemara hills stretch out to the left. Mystery also surrounds the numerous turloughs like the one at Carran. They fill up during the wet winter and retreat, decrease and almost disappear during a dry summer. Finally the underworld of caves, carved out over the millennia by underground streams, has its own beauty and magic as any visitor to the Aillwee caves can testify.

Thankfully, the visitor centre that the Office of Public Works (OPW) planned to build close to the mountain Mullaghmore will not go ahead. The argument has now been accepted that if one puts visitor centres in the middle of an area that is very sensitive, one risks destroying the beautiful site that draws people there in the first instance.

Still, this beautiful habitat has been seriously ravaged in recent years, through changes in agriculture and the increased impact of tourism. Writing to the *Irish Times* on 19 May 2000, Dr Richard Moles of the Department of Chemical and Environmental Sciences at Limerick University complained that in recent years 'much has changed for the worse, and the rate of deterioration is increasing'. He complained that 'species-rich heathland (rare in this part [around Mullaghmore] of the Burren) had been trampled and over-grazed into species-poor grassland marred by bare soil scars, and the soil is being washed away into holes in the limestone... Vegetation and soils are destroyed along tracks opened up by increasing numbers of hikers'.

Groves of aspen and other trees like birch and ash are unable to regenerate because of overgrazing by goats. In recent years I have seen vast areas of limestone being cleared and bulldozed, particularly east of Ballyvaughan. Instead of the variety of wildflowers that used to embellish the rock one now sees a thin layer of soil, planted with monotonous rye grass and the ubiquitous knapweed. One fears that it will only be a matter of time until holiday houses appear on this strip of land.

It seems to me that foreigners are sometimes more aware of the destruction that is taking place in the Burren than Irish people. Writing to the *Irish Times* on 16 August 2000 Geraldine Exton from Frankston in Australia called attention to the fad among tourists of building their cairns in Poulnabrone and in the process disturbing the fragile ecosystem.

Loss of Green Roads

I would like to see facilities put in place for people, Irish and overseas tourists, to enjoy the Burren without destroying it. This is why I am particularly upset when what are called the 'green-roads' are interfered with and are no longer accessible. In the area behind Fanore the sign for the green road has been removed and the entrance to the road behind Murroogh has been bulldozed. A newcomer, even with aid of Tim Robinson's map, would find it difficult to locate the beginning of the road. At the Ballyvaughan side of that walk the green road which Robinson shows leading down to the road does not, in fact, reach the highway. Similarly the green road that used to pass through Gleninagh South has been encroached upon so the right-of-way leading out over Gleninagh Pass is no longer accessible. Walking in Gleninagh in August 2000 I noticed that Mr Jim Donoghue was seeking permission to construct eight dwelling-houses with a sewerage treatment system at Gleninagh South. On inspecting the planning application 9656 at the courthouse in Ennis I was delighted to see that permission had been refused. If such holiday 'development' were allowed in the heart of the Burren it would truly mean the end of the Burren as we know it.

My question, which echoes Dr Mole's concerns in the *Irish Times* is as follows: is anyone systematically monitoring the widespread changes that are now taking place in the Burren and responding to them in an appropriate way? Are Clare or Galway Country Council or Dúchas capable of doing the job?

Is there a need for an area-wide Burren Authority to effectively protect this special area of Ireland and promote it in appropriate ways? I think that there is a dire need for such an agency. To really make a difference the agency would need to be well-resourced financially. The staff ought to be drawn from a variety of backgrounds. This might range from a conservation perspective for the flowers, birds and habitat to agriculture, tourism and local government. To function effectively the agency would need to develop a good working relationship with local communities, and various sectors in the community and with the Department of Agriculture and Tourism. Such an agency located in a town or village in the Burren could bring a creative and imaginative approach to making the Burren a better place to live in and visit while protecting its beauty and uniqueness for future generations.

Lough Derg

Lough Derg in the lower catchment area of the Shannon is the largest lake in the Republic of Ireland. I grew up on the outskirts of Nenagh, about five miles from Lough Derg. I have very pleasant memories of summers spent fishing and boating on the lake in the 1950s and 1960s.

Until the pattern of Irish agriculture changed in the 1960s, Lough Derg was renowned as a trout lake. The fact that trout will only thrive in rivers and lakes that enjoy good quality water indicates how healthy the lake was until the 1960s. Anglers from far and wide came, especially during the mayfly season. Dapping records kept by Ms Bruce of Lesseragh, Borrisokane, between 1904 and 1928 show a total catch of 44,495 trout of an average weight of 1.9 pounds.

Things changed with the industrialisation of Irish agriculture in the 1960s. Phosphate uses jumped from 20,000 tonnes in 1950 to 90,000 in the early 1970s followed by a decrease to roughly 60,000 tonnes per annum since. Slurry spreading, silage making and discharge from a variety of industrial plants has also added to the water pollution in Lough Derg.

It is little wonder then that by 8 August 1982 Donal Musgrave could write in the *Sunday Tribune* that 'Lough Derg has become a giant receptacle for human waste, industrial effluent, silage run-offs and turf mould from Midland bogs.' The article concluded that unless stringent measures were taken to reduce pollution Lough Derg could die within twenty or thirty years. A decade later the report of the Lough Derg Working Group published in September 1993 classified the lake as 'strongly eutrophic' and admitted that 'water quality in Lough Derg has been causing concern for years.'

Numerous reports have been published in the intervening years but little action has been taken. An algal bloom in August 2000 forced the North Tipperary County Council to erect signs stating that the water was unfit for bathing. Though numerous studies have been conducted in the past 20 years the level of pollution is still unacceptably high. On 31 August 2000 the *Irish Examiner* reported that 1,000 trout had been killed on the Abhann na Feorish river in Roscommon.

In general the source of the pollution is still human, agriculture and industrial waste. Some significant efforts have been made to reduce the pollution from human waste through the provision of tertiary sewage treatment plants. In the summer of 2000 Mr Paddy Mackey, secretary of the Save Our Lough Derg (SOLD) group, called for strict implementation of the By-Laws drawn up by County Councils in the catchment area dealing with nitrogen and phosphates entering the lake. Unless this happens the condition of Lough Derg will continue to deteriorate.

All farms in the catchment area, not just those in the Rural Environment Protection Scheme (REPS), should be required to submit a nutrient management plan. Naturally, farmers should be supported and compensated adequately for this service to the wider community and the environment. Animal slurry, soiled water and dairy washings can also be effectively treated by constructed wetlands. These artificially created wetlands emulate the ability of natural wetlands to purify water. Slurry has a very high Biochemical Demand (B.O.D.) which means that it can significantly deplete vital oxygen levels in water causing major problems for aquatic life. Effective sewage treatment plants and campaigns to use phosphate-free detergents are also vital if the Shannon waters are to be returned to their pristine state. Industry must also avoid polluting the river with hazardous waste or hazardous products.

There is no single solution to the problems faced by the Shannon and Lough Derg. Efforts have to be made on a number of fronts. The Lough Derg and Lough Rea Catchment Monitoring Group, which is jointly administered by Clare County Council and Roscommon County Council, is a very welcome initiative. The Management Proposals document was published in July 1999. The group includes ten County Councils and numerous statutory bodies. It espouses a catchment-based approach to 'reducing phosphorus inputs to rivers and lakes from all sources.' The Report 'undertakes to identify river stretches experiencing the effects of pollution, to catalogue the principal cause in each instance and to propose a range of key management measures which may be implemented by individual Local Authorities in problem areas.'[23] The primary sources of nutrient enrichment are industry, forestry and urban sewage and agriculture. Because it is diffuse, agricultural pollution is often more difficult to pinpoint and treat. Safe and adequate storage is needed for silage effluent, slurry, manure and dairy washings. Resources and programmes will need to be made available to farmers if these targets are to be met. The above Report estimates that '£30 million will be required to address farmyard problems in the priority risk area alone.'

While the Report is very thorough, I wonder whether its recommendations will be vigorously pursued by County Councils and Statutory Bodies. My reason for concern is that since the Toner et al[24] study of the Shannon in 1972 a host of other studies have taken place, but remedial action has been slow. The Lough Derg and Lough Rea Report acknowledges that there has been 'a deterioration in water quality [which] has endangered the general ecology of these waters and also reduced their value as public amenities particularly as a source of potable water' (p. 6).

At the moment, 13 County Councils and numerous semi-State and statutory bodies, often with conflicting agendas, have responsibility for the Shannon. One organisation, Dúchas, incorporates both the Board of Works and the Parks and Wildlife Service. The Board of Works has responsibility for drainage and navigation schemes while the Parks and Wildlife Service is responsible for conservation. These ends may often be in conflict.

The County Councils also do not have a great record in pursuing those who breach environmental laws. Take the one on hedgecutting. It is an offence to cut hedges between 1 April and 15 August. In 2000 I saw scores of people cutting hedges and, obviously destroying the habitat of birds, many of which are now endangered. To date there has not been a single prosecution.

What is needed is a single, well-resourced statutory body with responsibility for the complete Shannon basin. That would include the 14,700 km surveyed in the Lough Derg and Lough Rea Report. Membership of the Board of such a body ought to be based on a person's experience and qualifications rather than on affiliation to a particularly party. The numerous tribunals sitting at the moment make it abundantly clear that systems that promoted cronyism also facililate corruption. The goal of the body should be similar to that espoused by the Minister for the Environment: to restore the rivers to an unpolluted Class A status as defined by the EPA's biological quality classification system and for lakes to eliminate hypertrophic and eutropic conditions so as to achieve at least mesothrophic status (satisfactory conditions) (Report p 15).

We also need responsible political leadership if we are to deal effectively with water pollution. Unfortunately, this does not seem forthcoming in Ireland today. In early September 2000 we witnessed Ms Avril Doyle from Fine Gael and Gerry Collins from Fianna Fáil glorying in the fact that they had successfully lobbied the European commission to exempt Ireland from domestic water charges.[25]

There is also grave concern about the quality of ground water. A report from the Environmental Protection Agency (EPA) in March 1999 confirmed what many environmentalists knew, that 40 per cent of group water schemes in rural Ireland are contaminated with the E-coli bacteria which makes the water unfit for human consumption.[26] E-coli is a coliform. It can cause serious illnesses like gastro-enteritis in humans. Old people and children are particularly vulnerable.

An EU funded study conducted by Europe's leading experts on cyanobacteria found that 20 per cent of the lakes that it studied contained algal blooms which were caused by cyanobacteria.[27] An editorial in the *Irish Times* (7 January 2000) stated that 'cyanobacteria are among the most lethal substances known and can pose a severe threat to drinking water. They have been responsible for many animal deaths, and cause acute effects in humans, including skin conditions, vomiting and diarrhoea.' The Report acknowledges that 'it considered that the level of toxicity encountered substantially underestimated the true position.' Much of the eutrophication is caused by the excessive use of phosphate fertilisers, inappropriate slurry spreading and phosphates in household detergents. Little has been done in Ireland, to date, to effectively address any of these issues. Right through January 2000 I saw farmers spreading slurry on their lands.

The deteriorating situation with regard to Irish water is so serious that in January 2000 the European Commission decided to prosecute Ireland at the European Court for failing to provide safe drinking water for its citizens.[28] Again in September 2000 the European Commission warned the Irish Government that the pollution control measures introduced in the previous three years to address water pollution in Irish lakes and rivers were inadequate. The Commission has serious concerns about the phosphorus levels that have resulted in a decline in water quality since the 1970s.[29]

There is also concern about the purity of coastal waters. The Coast Watch report for 1997 complained that the excessive use of nitrate and phosphate fertilisers was polluting Ireland's coast to a 'very worrying' degree.[30]

Kilkee

Kilkee, situated on the Atlantic Ocean, is one of the best known resorts in the west of Ireland. The beautiful curve of the bay, Burn's Cove, the Pollock Holes, the Diamond rocks and the cliff walk all add their particular charm to this beautiful place. The history of Kilkee as a seaside resort goes back over two centuries. In 1793 the *Ennis Chronicle* advertised 'Kilkee House' as a suitable place for the bathing season.

There was quite a lot of building in Kilkee before the famine on the McDonnell estate at the west end. The Marquis of Conyngham, who owned land on the east side, had plans for ministered by An Taisce with financial support from the partment of the Environment. To receive the Blue Flag the ich must meet the criteria laid down in the EU Directive on ality of Bathing Waters and the Local Authority must ensure t adequate sanitary services and infrastructure are in place. e Local Authority must sample the water every two weeks ring the bathing season for faecal bacteria and other llutants.

Kilkee had a Blue Flag until 1995. It lost it between 1996 d 1998. The reason seemed to be that at least one of the two eams flowing across the beach – the Victoria Stream or the lantic Stream – was polluted. In the Summer of 1998 Clare unty Council erected a sign stating that 'This stream and the mediate vicinity is at present unsuitable for bathing or ddling due to recent high levels of bacteria. Please swim in proved designated area as indicated by buoys and signage.' hundred yards along the beach another sign read: 'Bathing rmitted'. At a public meeting called by the Planning Review oup in August 1998 the local GP told a packed hall that are County Council were obviously dealing with a very telligent bacteria that would avoid floating where the sign id no bathing.

In 1999 and again in 2000 I noticed that the mouth of the ctoria Stream was blocked up when I visited in June, July d August. Once in 1999, after a flood, the waters burst rough the dam. The structure in 2000 seemed more phisticated with something verging on a sluice mechanism. September 1999 and again in September 2000, the 12th to exact, the 'dam' was removed and the stream was allowed flow freely through the strand out to the sea. My question : what is the purpose of this 'dam'? Is it a way of dealing with e fact that the Victoria Stream is polluted? Is it about taining the Blue Flag? On 19 September I wrote to the eputy County Manager, Mr Tom Carey, raising these uestions. If any of these suggestions are correct, the Council

extensive building in the late 1850's. These never came to fruition and only two model houses were ever built. In the early part of the 20th century houses were built on the Mouth Charles Estate and 22 at McSweeney Terrace. Later in the 1970s, 78 houses were built in the Marian Estate. These houses are occupied all year round.

During the 1990s the face of Kilkee was transformed and deformed by a feverish building programme which was driven by tax inducements. I will argue here that the planning contravened three fundamental principles of planning namely, that it should be *ecologically sustainable, socially just and architecturally appropriate.*

Housing Boom

The number of houses in Kilkee prior to 1990 was 595, of which 428 were occupied all year round. This means that 71.9% of the housing stock was inhabited throughtout the year at that time. From 1992 to 1998 a total of 643 new houses were built in Kilkee. This is an increase of 132.77 per cent in the number of houses. Interestingly enough, the dramatic increase in housing has not lead to a massive increase in the permanent population. Of the 643 houses built, only 38 were built for permanent residents. Most of the houses that have been built are holiday houses and so are only occupied for a few months of the year. Those who occupy them then have very little permanent engagement with the community. At the moment only 34.25% of housing in Kilkee is inhabited all year round.

Inadequate sewage and water facilities

In contravention of any rational planning process the building spree took place with woefully inadequate sewage and water facilities. Even in 2001 Kilkee is still dependent on the sewage system that was upgraded in 1974. Untreated sewage is discharged into the ocean west of the town in Intrinsic Bay.

There is no definite plan to upgrade the present sewage system to meet the 2005 EU directive, which demands that untreated sewage should not be discharged into the ocean. In a letter dated 12 September 2000 the County Engineer, Mr T. Carey, stated that 'In the Council's Assessment of Needs of February 2000 the provision of sewage treatment in Kilkee was prioritised at No. 5. Unfortunately, Kilkee did not feature in the recently announced Water Service Investment Programme.'

The water system is also inadequate. During the summer months many residents of the Miltown Road and McSweeney Tce cannot take a shower until after midnight due to insufficient water pressure. In some households filling a kettle is quite tedious as the water comes in just a trickle. One household has bought four washing machines in a period of four years.

Houses have been built on almost every available scrap of land in the town. There is no provision for a public park, for sporting where some young person can kick a ball or puck a *sliotar* or play basketball during the long winter evenings.

St Joseph's Community College, the only secondary school in the peninsula, has a population of 335 students. The school has no gym, no hall, no track or playing pitch. If it were not for the local GAA, who have a pitch outside the town, there would be no facilities for young people at all. One does not need to be a social worker to realise that the lack of adequate playing and recreation facilities can contribute to young people experimenting with drugs and alcohol. The planning process seems to overlook these basic needs.

The influence of the building programme on the local economy is very significant. In 1998 a holiday home on the Miltown Road cost £140,000. A small number of houses in the Moore Bay complex were advertised for local purchase at £78,000. How can a local young couple buy a house at such inflationary prices? I do not know of any effective scheme either at the local, county or national level which is actually

addressing this kind of imbalance whic created by government sponsored tax br

I feel that one could justifiably mak socially unjust to favour well-off people community, and who contribute very lit with tax breaks to build holiday houses t the best part of the year at a time when social housing is being starved of public

Just looking at what has happened it planning authorities and the builders ha mind. Build as many houses as possible piece of land. Some houses that had a view mid-90s had this view completely obstructe of the building programme. The only view f is up into the sky.

Given the record of the past few years m every free spot in town has been built upor sanction a building programme for the mo on the coast road leading out to the Golleen habitat for choughs. They need lands tha closely cropped by cattle. If the present ha and replaced by houses with lawns in front mean the end of the chough population. B planners from sanctioning ribbon develop road? If the last ten years are anything to must be an emphatic no.

Beach

Kilkee, with its large circular beach of firm currents is an ideal spot for swimming, espe children. It is important for its tourist reputati resort like Kilkee retains its prestigious Blue Blue Flag scheme is an initiative of the Environmental Education in Europe (a netw government organisations). In Ireland t would be better off dealing with the pollution of the streams, rather than blocking them up. The dam was rebuilt in the summer of 2001.

Waste and the Disposable Society

The unsustainability and vulnerability of our present day global industrial and commercial society is very evident when one looks at it from the rubbish heaps which have continued to grow higher and higher in recent decades. A decade ago *Newsweek* (27 November 1989) portrayed the industrial world as being 'buried alive' in garbage.

Increased levels of waste are becoming a major problem in Ireland. In 1998 each individual generated half a tonne of waste. Between 1984 and 1995 there was a 62 per cent increase in the level of household and commercial waste.[31] 92 per cent of this waste ends up in landfills, but space is running out. The current situation is exacerbated by the phenomenal growth in the Irish economy during the past decade. It is estimated that waste has grown by at least 5 per cent per annum.[32]

Rates of recycling are very low in Ireland compared to other countries. An EPA Report in March 2000 indicated that 85% of paper was dumped in landfills and only 15% recycled, 70% of glass landfilled and only 30% recycled. The situation with metals is even worse. 95% ended in dumps and only 5% was recycled.[33] Despite efforts from local authorities and waste management companies to promote landfill and incineration options very few communities want a 'super dump' or an incinerator in their backyard. As I write the community in the picturesque village of Silvermines in North Tipperary is vigorously opposing the proposed mega-dump in their village. In the Republic we are just about to witness a major environmental battle around the siting of incinerators.[34]

Pope John Paul II has repeatedly made a connection between rampant consumerism and environmental destruction. In 1990 he wrote that:

> Modern society will find no solution to the ecological problem unless it takes a serious look at its lifestyle. In many parts of the world society is given to instant gratification and consumerism while remaining indifferent to the damage which these cause... simplicity, moderation and discipline as well as a spirit of sacrifice, must become part of everyday life, lest all suffer the negative consequences of the careless habits of a few.[35]

In Ireland there has been very little effort by religious leaders to promote recycling, re-using goods or simply cutting down on our use of material things and linking this lifestyle change to traditional Christian asceticism.

The Irish Environment

During the past 25 years increased industrialisation and intensive agriculture have taken a huge toll on the Irish environment. The EPA report for 1998 concedes that Ireland's environmental problems are intensifying with economic growth. Their main worry is that environmental degradation might scupper the 'Celtic Tiger'.[36]

One could continue to give depressing examples of global and national environmental destruction. My intention in presenting the data above is to give a valid framework which will help us to truly appreciate the level of environmental damage globally and locally. I believe it now threatens the survival of many of the earth's creatures in the short term, and includes human beings in the long term. We must now interpret and critique this devastation of the earth in the light of the Gospel and the resources of the Christian tradition.

Why are we so insensitive to environmental damage

To begin with we often fail to present an adequate context for understanding environmental damage. The most important thing when looking at the details of environmental devastation is to present it in an adequate context of understanding so that the implications of the data can be clearly appreciated. Unless this happens it is very easy to fall into what I call the litany approach to the environment. This merely lists environmental problems and adds them to a host of other woes like poor housing, unemployment, immigration, social tension, etc.

Such an approach trivialises the environmental issue for two reasons. Firstly, each new report of environmental damage is seen in isolation and thus the cumulative and global impact of what is happening can easily be missed. Looked at merely on a case by case basis, we can delude ourselves into thinking that ecological destruction is not a serious threat to life and that environmental campaigners are like the boy in the wolf story, simply trying to attract attention when there is no real danger.

Secondly, there is usually a time lag between environmentally destructive activity, like burning fossil fuel, and the moment when the resultant climate change is evident. No sane person will jump from a five-story building and hope to survive. The consequence of such a foolish action is clear and immediate. This, however, is not true in the domain of environmental problems like global warming, acid rain, ozone depletion, or mercury poisoning. It may be decades before the impact of our actions today, on the earth and the human community, is truly appreciated. Since our industrial society is focused on immediate gratification, this time lag permits politicians and communities to leave environmental issues to one side, or to address them through fine rhetoric, while resources are concentrated instead on tangible problems, like unemployment, industrial growth or inflation. The tragedy is that some of the accepted responses to today's problems, like promoting economic growth as a way of dealing with unemployment, can increase environmental damage in the long run and thus preclude the possibility for really good human work in a locality for decades or even centuries.

Ireland is very poorly served by the media when it comes to educating the public about the importance of environmental concerns. For example, there is no regular environmental programme on RTÉ television or radio. When I came home from the Philippines in the early 1990s there were two programmes I listened to each Saturday morning: *Scrap Saturday* followed by the environment programme. There was a hue and cry when *Scrap Saturday* was dropped but no agitation when the environment programme was discontinued. Radio One broadcasts *Mooney Goes Wild on One* on Sunday morning. I listen to this as often as I can but it is a naturalist, or natural history programme, rather than an environment programme.

The print media is even more forgetful of the environment. All Irish newspapers have supplements on a variety of subjects, sport, finance, fashion, property, farming, etc. The *Guardian* is the only newspaper in these islands that has a regular section on the environment. So despite protestations about the importance of the environment in their editorials, the actions or lack of actions speak much louder than their words.

On the political and administrative front the most important development in recent years was the establishment of the Environmental Protection Agency (EPA) on 26 July 1993. The EPA has a wide range of statutory duties and powers under the law. The non-governmental organisation (NGO) community at the time welcomed the establishment of the EPA. However, environmental NGOs were critical of the fact that sufficient

funds have not been made available so that the agency might
be really effective. At a structural level NGOs wondered how,
in a small community like Ireland where many people know
each other, an agency that granted IPC licences to industries
could effectively monitor and police these industries. They
made the point that it would be like asking Dáil deputies who
make laws to become judges in their own constituencies.

Despite green rhetoric, the environment is not a priority for
any political party in Ireland, apart from the Greens. For
example, in the course of an hour long speech at his party's
Ardfheis on October 13th 2001, the Taoiseach, Mr Bertie Ahern,
only devoted a single paragraph to concerns about the
enviroment. It is quite clear that it is not a top priority. Even
when environmental legislation is passed it is not always
implemented. The sad reality is that much of the response to
environmental degradation, for example, in the area of water
and waste, has been driven by EU Directives rather than the
Oireachtas.

We also lack a basic ethical framework that would heighten
our awareness of environmental destruction. Aristotle, whose
impact on Western thought is enormous, held the view that
since 'nature makes nothing without some end in view,
nothing to no purpose... It must be that nature has been made
for the sake of man.'[37] This idea that animals and plants are
created by God or some force for the exclusive benefit of
humankind has dominated western attitudes towards the rest
of creation for centuries.[38] Elements of the Judeo-Christian
tradition have strongly reinforced the Aristotelian legacy. Take
the Genesis 1: 26-28 text, 'Increase and multiply and dominate
the earth'. This text has often been interpreted, mistakenly
according to contemporary scripture scholars, as giving
humans a licence to dominate the earth and do whatever they
wish to animals and plants.

It is true that within the Judaeo-Christian tradition there has
been a strand that saw humans as stewards of Creation (Gen

2:15). Unfortunately, as the historian Clives Ponting points out in his *Green History of the World*, although the idea that humans have a responsibility to preserve the natural world of which they are merely guardians can be traced through a succession of thinkers, it has remained a minority tradition. Unfortunately, St Francis' kinship with Brother Sun, Sister Moon and the rest of creation was such a minority position. It did not inform Western approaches to nature during the centuries that followed.

Recent Catholic Church Teaching on the Environment

Despite the destruction that is taking place in our world, the Churches have not responded in any effective way to environmental destruction. Let me illustrate what I am saying by a few quotations from recent Catholic Church teaching.

Vatican II is undoubtedly the major achievement of the Catholic Church in the twentieth century. *Gaudium et Spes* (The Pastoral Church in the Modern World) is a milestone in the history of the Church's stance towards the world. It embodies a positive, liberating vision of life that refuses to seal off religious issues from the rest of human affairs. One cannot, however, argue that it is grounded in an ecological vision of reality. This document subscribes to what is called 'dominion theology'; the natural world is there for man's exclusive use, 'for man, created in God's image, received a mandate to subject to himself all that it contains, and govern the world with justice and holiness' (No. 34).

This anthropocentric bias is even more marked in No. 12 of the same document. It claims almost universal agreement for the teaching that 'according to the unanimous opinion of believers and unbelievers alike, all things on earth should be related to man as their centre and crown.' The cultures of tribal peoples and Hinduism and Buddhism, the great religions of the East, can hardly be used to bolster up this claim.

The first papal document devoted exclusively to environment and development issues, entitled *Peace with God the Creator, Peace with all Creation,* was published on 1 January 1990. In it the Pope draws attention to the moral and religious dimensions of the environmental crisis. He declares that 'Christians in particular realise that their duty towards nature and Creator are an *essential* part of their faith' (No. 15 emphasis mine). This teaching is arguably the best kept secret in the Catholic Church globally, and here in Ireland I have seldom heard it being quoted.

It is also important to acknowledge that this document is heavily dependent on the Justice, Peace and Integrity of Creation (JPIC) programme which the World Council of Churches launched at its Assembly in Vancouver in 1983. To its credit the World Council of Churches is one of the few Christian institutions that has consistently focused its attention on ecology, development, justice and poverty during the past 25 years. It is a pity that the two most recent encyclicals – *Evangelium Vitae* (Gospel of Life) and *Fides et Rationis* (Faith and Reason) are so engrossed in human problems and moral challenges that they barely mention the current ecological crisis.

Given that the Christian Churches have arrived at these challenges a little breathless and a little late, they must now make up for lost time and, in co-operation with other faiths throw all their energies into urgently addressing the challenge of the JPIC. Unless this awareness is gained in the very near future human beings and the rest of the planet's community will be condemned to live amid the ruins of the natural world.

How the Churches might respond to environmental ruin?

The first and most important contribution that the Churches could make to the present ecological crisis would be to acknowledge the magnitude of the problem and urge people to face it with courage. Much of the data regarding the deteriorating state of our air, water, soils and tropical forests is now generally accepted by the scientific community.

Need for a prophetic witness from the Churches

Yet many Northern governments and, especially transnational corporations, who have benefitted from the current shape of the global economy, are unwilling to acknowledge the extent of the problem and as a consequence to change their ways. The inability of politicians at a national and global level to tackle the issue effectively is a case in point. As we saw earlier the 2,000 scientists of Intergovernmental Panel on Climate Change (IPCC) called for a 60 per cent cut in emission of greenhouse gases in an effort to lessen the full impact of global warming. Corporate interests, especially in the coal, oil and automobile sectors, have lobbied very effectively to block any increase in taxes on fossil fuel or any serious effort to reduce greenhouse gas emissions in the US to 1990 levels by the year 2,010. In the run-up to the Climate Change Convention in Kyoto in December 1997 the United States Congress resisted any initiative on a carbon tax. So while scientists are painting appalling scenarios, politicians, manipulated by the corporate world, are willing to adopt a wait-and-see attitude.

In the face of these efforts to downplay the seriousness of the climate change issue, the Churches must be resolute in their determination to witness to the truth. To date, the Churches have often taken a so-called 'balanced' position or have remained silent on ecological issues in order not to fall out with those who wield economic or political power. Such even-handedness is difficult to square with the Gospel call for a clear stance on the side of the poor and the exploited earth. This is the heart of the Church's prophetic responsibility. One is reminded of the responsibility of the watchman in the book of Ezekiel to alert the community in the time of danger.

> But if the watchman sees the sword coming and does
> not blow the trumpet, so that people are warned, and
> the sword comes, and takes any one of them; that man
> is taken away in his iniquity, but his blood I will
> require of the watchman's hand. (Ezek.33:6)

The World Council of Churches has responded to this crisis by publishing a very thorough analysis of the ecological, economic, ethical, theological and pastoral aspect of global warming in a document called *Accelerated Climate Change: Sign of Peril, Test of Faith.*[39] The text discusses the theological and ethical issues involved in global warming and attempts to motivate the Churches to become involved in the issue. All the Christian Churches should throw their moral authority behind this document. It is worth remembering that while Church presence was very evident at the United Nations conference on population in Cairo (1995), there was hardly a word from religious leaders before, during or since Kyoto (December 1997), despite the misery that global warming will create.

Toward a theology and spirituality of creation

Another important contribution that the Churches can make is to develop a spirituality of creation. In attempting to do this Christian thinkers will find many helpful insights both in the biblical tradition and in different Christian spiritualities which have flourished, often it must be admitted at the margins, during the past two millennia. One thinks of the centrality of creation in both Celtic spirituality and the spirituality of St Francis of Assisi.

If this theology is to focus on the well-being of the total biosphere, or in theological terms, on all God's creation, then it will have to adopt what the Australian biblical theologian, Elaine Wainwright, has called a 'hermeneutics of reclamation', simply because much of the classical Christian tradition is very human centred.[40]

Genesis calls us to imitate a gracious God who loves Creation and cares for the Earth

One could begin this 'hermeneutic of reclamation' right at the first line of Genesis. The Bible affirms that the world was created by a personal God who declares that it is good and who loves His creation (Gen 1:1). This is an extremely important statement as many cultures in the ancient Near East believed that, since the Earth was subject to decay, it must have been created, at least, in part, by an evil spirit. This belief still lingers on even in the minds of people who profess to be Christian. It is one of the reasons why people who claim to be Christians can lay waste a forest or destroy fragile ecosystems without having the slightest twinge of conscience that what they are doing might be wrong.

The divine injunction to humankind in Gen 1:28 'to increase and multiply and have dominion over the earth' is not a licence to exploit creation. Nowadays scripture scholars argue that the commission, and especially the notion of dominion, originally was understood as a challenge to humans to imitate God's loving kindness and faithfulness and act as his viceroy in regard to the non-human component of the earth. Like the viceroys of the king, men and women are expected to be just, honest and render real service. The virtues of the righteous king are portrayed in Ps 72: 4-6. He will combine defence of the poor: 'may he defend the cause of the poor' (verse 4) with concern for the fertility of the land; 'may he be like rain that falls on the mown grass, like showers that water the earth' (verse 6). In the Psalms (e.g. Ps 104) and Wisdom literature, especially the Book of Job, there is a clear appreciation that the raison d'être of creation is not found primarily in its ability to meet human needs. It has its own dignity, its own rights and reasons for being, quite apart from its role in sustaining humans. This is stated very clearly in the speeches of Yahweh in the book of Job chapters 38-41. Creation has intrinsic value because it is created by God and sustained by God's Spirit.

Furthermore there is a strong sense of the interdependence of all creatures in Psalm 104. Ian Bradley in *God is Green* writes that in the Bible 'God is seen as the Lord of all creation' and that 'there is a strong sense of the interdependence of all creatures and an image of the world as of a single cosmic community rather than [as] a collection of autonomous entities.'[41]

Stewardship

A theology of creation will also have to deal with the fact that human well-being, both for individuals and communities, depends on other creatures and a fertile environment. Here again the Bible has much to teach us in regard to how we relate to the rest of creation. In chapter two and three of the Book of Genesis humans are challenged to be stewards of God's creation and to live in companionship with the rest of creation. The command of God to Adam and Eve is 'to till and to keep' (Gen 2:15).

For the people of Israel the demands of stewardship are seen in the sensitive way they viewed the land. Aware of their origins as nomads and outcasts, they saw the land as a gift from God. Among the neighbours of Israel, the land was often seen as the exclusive property of the king or ruling classes (1 Kings 21). This was not true in Israel. Land was the heritage of all the people and it was meant to sustain the whole community (Ex 19:5). But in a deeper way Israel knew that she did not, in fact, own the land. Yahweh was the true land owner. The cultivators were only God's tenants; they were stewards and it was clearly recognised that there were certain restrictions on how they might utilise it:

> The land must not be sold in perpetuity, for the land belongs to me and to me you are only strangers and guests (Lev 25:23).

The stewardship metaphor has sometimes been criticised as being excessively human-centred and too simplistic for addressing complex ecological challenges.[42] Despite these reservations the ideas and attitudes involved in stewardship have much to teach this generation which feels there is a technological answer to all environmental challenges. Modern mechanized agriculture that exploits land to the point of exhaustion in order to maximise short-term profits has much to re-learn from the wisdom contained in book of Leviticus.

> I have come that they may have life and have it to the full (Jn 10:10).

A Christian theology of creation begins with the reality of the incarnation. This affirms that God became not merely a human being but a part of all creation. One difficulty with the theology of the incarnation almost from the beginning was that it tended to emphasis the divinity of Christ rather than his humanity. As a consequence many patristic authors taught that God became human to make humans divine 'not to celebrate but to overcome the frailties of the flesh that tied it to corruptibility and death.'[43]

Even a cursory reading of the Gospels reveals that Christians have much to learn from the attitude of respect that Jesus displayed towards the natural world. He enjoyed an intimacy with nature which is evident from his parables – the sower and the seed (Mt 13:4-9, 18-23), the vine and the branches (Jn 15:1-17; Mk 12:1-12). He illustrated his stories by referring to the lilies of the field (Lk 12:27), the birds of the air (Mt 6:26) and foxes and their lairs (Lk 9:58).

In this age of unbridled consumerism, where greed is often represented as a virtue, it is important to remember that Jesus lived lightly on the Earth. He warned his disciples against hoarding possessions and allowing their hearts to be enticed by the lure of wealth (Mt 6:19-21). It is clear that we will find no support in the teachings of Jesus for the modern throw-away, earth destroying consumer society.

One of the most striking features of the ministry of Jesus in St Mark's gospel is that he spoke with authority and the people listened (Mk 1:26). Jesus did not tailor his message to meet the expectation of any particular constituency. He communicated the truth about the situation of his time and invited people to respond by changing their behaviour, repenting their sinfulness so that the reign of God might break into the world. Recognising that human sin has destroyed not just human bonds but the fabric of creation is an essential dimension in proclaiming the Good News in today's world. As should be clear from the first part of this presentation the 'groaning of creation' which Paul writes about in Romans 8:22 has never been as extensive or as shrill. So, protecting and restoring creation must be at the heart of promoting the reign of God. The Christian Churches, as the midwives of this reign, must speak the truth about global environmental destruction in a much more forthright and unambiguous way. They must also encourage new possibilities of living that are much less destructive. The theological pathways to achieving this reconciliation in the Christian tradition are through imitating the self-emptying and unselfishness of Christ. As is clear from Col 1.20 and Eph 2.26 this will often involve pain and the way of the cross. It will involve standing with victims, including the suffering earth against the architects of destruction.

For contemporary Christian living it is important to remember that the centrality of Jesus is not confined to reflecting on his behaviour during his short life on earth in Palestine. We are resurrection people. Jesus is, as Paul tells us in Col 3:11, Eph 1:9-10 and many similar texts, the centre of human and cosmic history.

Jesus as the Word and Wisdom of God was active before the dawn of time bringing creation to birth out of the chaos. Through him the Universe, the Earth, and all life was created (Jn 1:3-5). All the rich unfolding of the universe, from the initial glow of the fireball through the shaping of the stars and the earth as the green planet of the universe, right up to the emergence of humans and their varied cultures and histories is centred on Jesus (Col 1:16-17).

In *The God of Evolution* the Australian theologian Denis Edwards recalls the Christology of Karl Rahner, one of the more insightful Catholic theologians of the twentieth century. Rahner argues that viewed from the Divine perspective Jesus is the ultimate, irreversible self-communication of God with humankind, all other creatures and the entire universe. Looked at from the Earth and Human perspective Jesus is the definitive Human-Earth acceptance of this communication. Edwards summarises Rahner by stating that 'In Jesus, God gives God's self to the evolving world in love and irrevocably; in Jesus, the evolving creation accepts God definitively and irrevocably.'[44]

Edwards develops a profound Trinitarian theology in the light of modern science and the ecological crisis. He argues that the most fruitful way of understanding the Divine today is as a God of mutual and equal relations. 'If God is Being-in-Relation, then this provides a basis for thinking about reality as radically relational. A relational ontology provides a meeting point for Christian theology and evolutionary biology. In Christian theology, the relational Trinitarian God can be understood as making space within the divine relations for a dynamically unfolding universe and for the evolution of life in all its diversity and interconnectedness.'[45] Understanding God as Trinity means that we view the Divine reality primarily in relational terms. We know from the insights of modern physics and biology that all reality is primarily relational. Creation in this perspective is understood as a community of beings interconnected with each other and with the triune God. Our way of relating within such an interdependent world must be through mechanisms or *koinonia* (community) rather than through dominant or exploitative behaviour.

Finally, Christians often make the mistake of thinking that the resurrection somehow catapults Jesus out of the order of creation and places him in some atemporal zone. The New Testament is adamant that the Risen Christ is even more deeply centred in all creation. The preface for the Mass of Easter Day rejoices in the fact that the resurrection 'renews all creation'. In the context of extinction it is important to remember that every living creature on earth has a profound relationship with the resurrected Lord. His loving touch heals our brokenness and fulfils all creation. So, to wantonly destroy any aspect of creation or to banish forever any species from their place in the community of life is to deface the image of Christ which is radiated throughout our world. Christ still suffers not only when people are denied their rights and exploited but when seas, rivers and forests are desecrated. As the Australian theologian Norman Habel puts it, 'God is found in weakness, in suffering, in servant earth.'[46]

An Earth Spirituality

The Bible vigorously denies that the world is evil. In Chapter one of Genesis, God repeatedly contemplates what he has created and 'sees that it is good' (Gen 1:10, 18, 19, 21a and 26). It also affirms that the God, whom we experience in our lives, is not hiding in some inaccessible part of the Universe. Creation is alive with the presence of God, if like the Psalmist, we look at it through the eyes of Faith:

> The heavens are telling the glory of God;
> And the firmament proclaims his handiwork.
> Day to day pours forth speech,
> And night to night declares knowledge (Ps 19. 1-2).

The prophet Isaiah is convinced that 'the whole earth is full of God's glory' (Isa 6.3)

I believe an authentic creation spirituality would help regenerate Irish Christianity and, especially, Irish Catholicism. Celtic spirituality celebrated the goodness of God that was manifested in the beauty of the world around us. Many Celtic monasteries were sited in remote and beautiful places like Skellig and Iona. It is no wonder that the monks came to love the cry of the curlew, the flight of the gannet, the bark of seals, the beauty of trees and wild flowers and the buzzing of bees and insects.

This love of creation and ability to find God in creation is also present in Celtic art. Fr Gerard Rice makes this point in his review of the CD-ROM of the Book of Kells in a recent article in the pastoral journal, *The Furrow*. According to Rice, the scribe directs our attention to the chi-rho sign. These first two Greek letters of Christ's name superimposed on each other was a common way of referring to Christ in the early church. The chi-rho dominates the page and grasps the attention of the reader. The text on the page carries the first line of Matthew's gospel, which begins with the words *Christi Generatio* – the genealogy of Christ. By deftly juxtaposing the text and the illustrations the scribe wishes to affirm that the birth of Christ is good news not just for men and women but for all of God's creation. The total effect of the experience is to echo St Paul's thought in Romans 8:22-24.

> Creation still retains the hope of being freed like us, from the slavery to decadence, to enjoy the same freedom and glory as the children of God. From the beginning till now, the entire creation, as we know, has been groaning

in one great act of giving birth, and not only creation
but all of us, the first fruits of the Spirit, we too groan
inwardly, as we wait for our bodies to be set free.

To bolster his case, Rice points to the illustration on the left
side, of an otter eating a fish (the Greek word *Ichthus*, a fish,
was traditionally understood as an acronym for Jesus Christ,
Son of God and Saviour). This convergence of the text and the
illustrations proclaims that nature is nourished by the
Saviour's birth. As if that were not enough there is a cartoon
portraying two mice feeding on the host, calmly observed by
their traditional enemy – two cats – and finally the cats carry
rats on their shoulders. Rice feels that the illustrator is
drawing on the vision of peace and harmony envisaged by
Isaiah in chapter 11:6-9 when 'the wolf shall dwell with the
lamb'.

Rice goes on to link this Celtic understanding of the role of
Christ in bringing peace to all creation to the doctrine of the
cosmic Christ. It has been generally thought that John
Eriugena, the Celtic philosopher who taught at the court of
Charles the Bald, elaborated the doctrine of the cosmic Christ
after reading the works of the Greek Fathers Gregory of Nyssa
and Gregory Nazianzen. But, as is clear from the discussion
above, this doctrine appears in a visual form in the Book of
Kells, which predates Eriugena's presence at the court by at
least a half a century. Rice is convinced that 'Eriugena's
enthusiasm for the Pauline doctrine owed as much to the
attitude which shaped the pre-Christian life of his ancestors –
the holiness of created things which for Christians derives
from the incarnation of Christ, who made all things sweet
again – as it did to his reading the Greek Fathers of the
Church.'[47]

This traditional Celtic sensitivity to the presence of God in the
world is also found in Joseph Mary Plunkett's beautiful poem 'I
See His Blood Upon the Rose'.

I see his blood upon the rose
and in the stars the glory of his eyes,
his body gleams amid eternal snows,
his tears fall from the skies.

I see his face in every flower;
the thunder and the singing of the birds
are but his voice – and, carven by his power
rocks are his written words.
All pathways by his feet are worn,
his strong heart stirs the ever-beating sea,
his crown of thorns is twined in every thorn,
his cross is every tree.[48]

Such a spirituality has much wisdom to offer to modern Ireland. It reminds us that we do not have a right to dominate and exploit nature without a thought for the consequences for other creatures and future generations.

Many Irish poets point in a similar direction. The last sentence of Patrick Kavanagh's poem 'The One' ('...breathing His love by a cut-away bog.') captures that special sense of God that comes to us in the few areas of relative wilderness that survive in modern Ireland.

We need to remember that when we pollute, scar and destroy creation either locally or globally we diminish the capacity of all people of faith to discern God's presence in creation. If this destruction is irreversible it is particularly poignant because the damage to faith is also permanent.

Renewing Liturgy and Devotions

The Church should recognise the transformative power that liturgy and worship have in shaping individual and community values that promote justice and the integrity of creation. Good ritual can help communities evolve a new mode of human interaction with other human beings and with the natural world. Since the emergence of humankind on earth people have always sought to link the deepest mysteries of their own personal and community life with the rhythms of the earth and cosmos through myths, rituals and ceremonies.

Sacraments

The sacramental liturgy of the Church offers many moments in which the Christian community can experience the presence of God in the world of nature. This sacramental approach to religion is central to both the Catholic and Greek Orthodox experience. Humans are called to be a blessing for other human beings and the rest of creation. In recent times this radical, sacrificial commitment to the welfare of others has been restated by the Ecumenical Patriarchate in a document called *Orthodoxy and the Ecological Crisis.*

> At the centre of worship is the Eucharist. The Eucharist is also the most sublime expression and experience of creation transformed by God the Holy Spirit through redemption and worship. In the form of bread and wine, material from creation, moulded into new forms by human hands, is offered to God with the acknowledgement, spelt out... that all creation is God's and that we are returning to God that which is His. In the sense that this captures the primordial relationship of Adam to both God and Creation it is a sign of the restoration of that relationship, and even more than that, a foretaste of the eschatological state of creation. When we partake of the body and blood of Christ, God meets us in the very substance of our relationship with creation and truly enters into the being of our biological existence.
>
> From this we know that humanity occupies the most special place in all creation – but is not the whole of creation. We know that as all is from God... we must respect creation and acknowledge that we are not its owners, but the ones who may enhance it by the use of our technology and skill, only however so as to

> offer it again to its creator... Just as a priest at the
> Eucharist offers the fullness of creation and receives it
> back as the blessing of Grace in the form of the
> consecrated bread and wine, to share with others, so
> we must be the channel through which God's grace
> and deliverance is shared with all creation. The human
> being is simply yet gloriously the means of expression
> of creation in its fullness and the coming of God's
> deliverance for all creation.[49]

The servant and sacramental model developed here in the
Ecumenical Patriarchate can also inspire a Catholic,
sacramental approach to creation.

Baptism

In the Catholic liturgy we are incorporated into the Church
through the sacrament of baptism. The symbolism of baptism
revolves around life-giving water and the power of the Spirit to
transform the lives of individuals and whole communities. This
ought to act as a strong incentive for the Christian community
to ensure that their water and the waters in their locality are not
polluted with toxic, human, industrial and agricultural waste.
Baptism initiates people into the Christian community, but I feel
that at this point in human and planetary history we must
expand the boundaries of what we understand as our
community to include all the community of the living. Studies
in recent decades in biology and evolution have expanded our
knowledge of the place of humans within the wider earth-
community. As we have seen above, ecological data across a
broad spectrum has confirmed the extensive destruction of this
community at the hands of humans. It would be helpful if in
administering the sacrament of baptism we saw it as not merely
initiating people into the Catholic Church, but as initiating
them also into the wider earth and cosmic community.

Christ's own baptism in the Jordan is linked to his mission
to bring about justice and peace for all: 'In the waters of the

Jordan your Son was baptised by John and anointed by the Spirit.' Fr Killian McDonnell writes about the cosmic dimension of the baptism of Jesus. He recalls the picture by Gregory Nazianzen, who has Jesus 'carrying the cosmos with him as he ascends out of the water of the Jordan.' He goes on to argue that 'the cosmic dimensions of the baptism of Jesus are part of antiquity's broader conviction, rooted in incarnation and resurrection, that the material universe, as the home of a redeemed humanity, is destined for transfiguration through the power of the Spirit manifested in the risen body of Christ.'[50]

McDonnell is very aware that the unity between creation and the cosmos and their common destiny raises questions about pollution, the depletion of the ozone layer, the waste of natural resources, the denuding of our forests, the contamination of our rivers, the release of harmful agents into the air.

He goes on to argue that the 'ecological movement should have as its goal not only the preservation and restoration of the natural environment because we live and die here. Creation should be worthy of its vocation to praise. "Praise him, sun and moon... Praise the Lord... mountains and all hills, fruit trees and all cedars! Wild animals and all cattle, creeping things and flying birds"' (Ps 148). The cosmos lives in hope. The Universe is destined for God and for transformation. As the cosmos has a true historical past with God, which is part of 'anamnesis', the cosmos has a real future in God.[51]

Eucharist

The Eucharist is also pregnant with all kinds of creative possibilities for deepening our awareness of the holy communion that unites God, humankind, other creatures and all creation. In the Eucharist the elements of Bread and Wine, taken from the Earth and transformed by human labour, are offered in memory of the Passion, Death and Resurrection of Jesus, and through the action of the Spirit they are transformed into the Body and Blood of Christ. The experience of Eucharist is a spur to Christians to work for a just, compassionate, sharing society. It also summons Christians to work for a sustainable society where seeds and soils are protected and the bonds of interdependence between humans and the rest of creation are more clearly understood and experienced. The Eucharist is that holy communion in which all the members give themselves to one another in order to promote abundant life for all.

Promoting and preparing for a new, sustainable culture

Moving beyond liturgy, environmental issues must become part of the wider pastoral ministry of the Church. It is sad and ironic that the present ecological crisis is the result of considerable human ingenuity. Everyone will admit that greed, covetousness and other commonly recognised human vices have undoubtedly contributed to our present crisis. Nevertheless, the principal cause of ecological devastation in our world today has been the unrelenting pursuit of what many people consider a good and desirable thing – the modern, growth-oriented, industrial model of development. What many people feel is the good life, something to be aspired to and worked for, is in fact destroying the world. The *Guardian* correspondent George Monbiot made a telling point in a recent article. He was reflecting on comments made by the Princeton physicist Freeman Dyson that the planet Mars could be made habitable within the next 50 years by planting genetically engineered trees there. The Princeton professor argued that this could facilitate space tourism and encourage the export of 'surplus population' to protect the earth from ecological disaster. As Monbiot points out 'his plan threatens to precipitate the very catastrophe he wants to avoid.'[52]

On a local level the economic boom in Ireland since the mid-1990s, with GDP growth rates of between 6 and 9 per cent, has taken a huge toll on the environment. Even someone like the former Taoiseach, Dr Garret FitzGerald, 'whose interest lies more in the economic field than the ecological one' believes that 'the Celtic tiger threatens to devour Ireland's much-hyped pristine environment' (*Irish Times* 26 May 1997).

The Churches must work assiduously with all those who are attempting to oppose this destructive way of living and espouse a more compassionate and sustainable culture that will support and enhance all life. The Dominican Sisters are to be commended for not selling 70 acres of prime land in the vicinity of Wicklow. Instead they have transformed it into a biodynamic enterprise with a wild-life sanctuary and an ecology centre.[53] It would be a wonderful millennial initiative if other religious orders who still own land followed this creative example.

To date, only one Irish bishop, Bishop Bill Murphy of Kerry, has tackled the environmental issue in a pastoral letter.[54] Given the environmental challenge globally and nationally, the fact that the leadership of the Irish Church has not addressed its moral and religious implications is in my mind a major failure in terms of effective episcopal leadership.

The Irish bishops could perform a great service both for the Irish people and the environment by initiating a national dialogue about the environment. This process ought to be carried out on an ecumenical basis. The Pope's 1990 letter recognises the potential for 'a vast field of ecumenical and inter-religious co-operation' around environmental questions. Such discussion at local and national level might well flower into a powerful pastoral letter.

The work to be done

As each year passes we are becoming more aware of how much damage this generation of human beings has done – and is doing – to all the ecosystems of the planet. Even the environment in Ireland, which our tourist literature proclaims as clean and green, has been abused in recent decades. The water in our streams and wells, for example, is no longer potable.

We know that no single generation has the right to use up all the fossil fuel in the world and generate global warming, erode all the topsoil, deplete the ozone layer, build up nuclear waste, poison streams and oceans and destroy tropical forests in order to secure an affluent lifestyle for a mere one-fifth of humanity. Future generations, our children's children, have the right to inherit a world as fertile and beautiful as the world we inherited.

Pope John Paul, in his January 2001 statement which I quoted already, calls for an 'ecological conversion'. This will inevitably involve personal and community sacrifices as we attempt to live more lightly on the earth. Religious traditions all over the world can help give people the vision and energy to respond to the challenge of protecting our environment and caring for the Earth. In this pamphlet I have argued that as Christians and Catholics we should be in the forefront of this great work for two reason. Firstly, we believe that, in the person of Jesus, God became incarnate in our world and thus became part of the Earth community. No action of ours should ever be allowed to destroy the face of Christ as revealed in creation. Secondly, as Catholics, we experience the presence of God in natural realities like bread, wine, water and oil. This should spur us, both individually and as a Church that has a local and global presence, to use all the insights we can glean from any quarter to love, respect and protect God's creation.

Notes

1   Sean McDonagh, *Passion for the Earth*, London, Chapman, 1994, pp. 1-2.

2   Paul Brown, 'The dilemma that confronts the world', *Guardian*, 16 September 1999, p. 3.

3   Pope John Paul II, 'God made man the steward of creation', L'Osservatore Romano, 24 January 2001, p. 11

4   Paul Brown, op. cit.

5   Tim Radford, 'Wearing the World Away', *Guardian*, 5 March 1995

6   Adela Gooch, 'Orchard of Spain crumbles into dust', *Guardian*, 25 May 2000, p. 21.

7   David Cabot, Ireland, London, HarperCollins, 1999, pp. 423-4

8   The Prince of Wales, 'We must go with the grain of nature', *The Times*, 18 May 2000

9   Julian Borger 'Banned GM corn reported in taco snack', *Guardian*, 19 September 2000, p. 17

10   Cathryn Atkinson, 'Seeds of Doubt', *Guardian*, 2 February 2000, p. 4

11   Juliette Terzieff 'Romania counts the cost of cyanide river disaster', *Sunday Times*, 20 February 2000, p. 27

12   Don Hinrichsen 'The Ocean Planet', *People and Planet*, 1998, p. 6-7

13   Dr William Reville, 'Water, water everywhere - but not for everyone', *Irish Times*, 15 May 2000, p. 9

14   Donal Hickey, *Irish Examiner*, 28 August 2000, p. 15; and Treacy Hogan 'Crucial facts on water pollution were held back' Irish Independent, 22 September 2001, p. 3

15   Eugene Liden Churchill, 'The Big Meltdown', *Time*, 4 September 2000

16   Dr Mick Hulme 'There is no longer such a thing as a purely natural weather event', *Guardian*, 15 March 2000, p. 4

17   Tim Radford, 'Melting Arctic will mean chillier Britain', *Guardian*, 7 April 2000, p. 9

18   Tim O'Brien, 'State Faces penalties over greenhouse gas emissions', *Irish Times*, 26 August 2000, p. 5

19   Treacy Hogan, 'Greenhouse gases head for twice agreed levels' *Irish Independent*, 28 April 2000, p. 10

20   Polly Toynbee, 'Going up in smoke', *Guardian*, 28 September 2000, p. 15

21 Frank McDonald, 'Adoption of Kyoto Protocol by the US is Vital', *Irish Times*, 18 November 2000, p. 9

22 Treacy Hogan and Kathy Donaghy, 'Car Free Days "a recipe for traffic chaos" says AA', *Irish Independent*, 30 August 2000

23 Lough Derg and Lough Rea Catchment Monitoring and Management System, Consultants Kirk McClure Morton, 40 Upper Grand Canal Street, Dublin

24 P.F. Toner, K.J. Clabby and J.J. Bowma,'Report on the Results of a Biological and Chemical Survey of the Main River Channel and Lakes of the Shannon System between Battle Bridge and Killaloe, Undertaken in July 1972', An Foras Forbartha, 1973

25 Conor Sweeny, 'Households to escape EU water charges ruling', *Irish Independent*, 6 September 2000

26 Liam Reid, 'E-coli in 40% of rural tap water', *Sunday Tribune*, 7 March 1999, p. 1

27 Kevin O'Sullivan, 'Danger of toxic microbes in Irish Lakes highlighted', *Irish Times*, 5 January 2000, p. 5

28 Treacy Hogan, 'Pollution risks land Dempsey in hot water', *Irish Independent*, 12 January 2000

29 Eithne Donnellan, 'State warned again over poor pollution response', *Irish Times*, 13 September 2000

30 Frank McDonald, 'Nitrate and phosphate over-use is blamed for coastal pollution', *Irish Times*, 3 December 1997, p. 10

31 Kevin O'Sullivan, 'Problems of the environment are intensifying-EPA', *Irish Times*, 15 July 1999, p. 14

32 Liam Reid, 'Ireland's dumps are full', *Sunday Tribune*, 30 January 2000, p. 9

33 Treacy, Hogan, 'Celtic Tiger drowning in its own waste say experts', *Irish Independent*, 23 March 2000, page 5.

34 Treacy Hogan 'Growing ire over a burning issue' Irish Independent, 25 January 2000, p. 13

35 'Peace with God the Creator, Peace with all Creation', *L'Osservatore Romano*, 1 January 1990

36 Kevin O'Sullivan, 'Problems of the environment are intensifying –EPA', *Irish Times*, 15 July 1999, p. 14

37 *Aristotle, Politics*, Harmondsworth, Penguin, 1985

38 Clive Ponting, *A Green History of the World*, Sinclair-Stevenson, 1991, p. 142

39 'Signs of Peril, Test of Faith: Accelerated Climate Change', World Council of Churches, 150 Route de Ferney, PO Box 2100, 1221 Geneva 2, Switzerland, May 1994

40 Elaine Wainwright, 'A Metaphorical Walk through Scripture in an Ecological Age', *Pacafica*, Summer 1994, PO Box 271, Brunswick East, Victoria 3057, Australia

41 Ian Bradley, *God is Green*, Longman, Darton and Todd, 1992, p. 19

42 Clare Palmer 'Stewardship: a case study in environmental ethics' in Ian Hall, Margaret Goodall, Clare Palmer and John Reader (eds), T*he Earth Beneath: A Critical Guide to Green Theology*, London, SPCK, 1992

43 Rosemary Radford Ruether, 'Sex and the Body in the Catholic Tradition', *Conscience* [A Newsjournal of Pro-choice Catholic Opinion], Winter 1999/2000, quoting *Athanasius One, the Incarnation of the Word Religious Tract Society*, London, 1903

44 Denis Edwards, *The God of Evolution*, New York, Paulist Press/Mahwah, NJ, 1999, p. 107

45 Ibid., p. 126

46 Norman Habel, 'Key Ecojustice Principles', in *Ecotheology*, Sheffield Academic Press, 1998, p. 120

47 Gerard Rice, 'The Book of Kells', *Furrow*, July/August 2001, p. 400-401

48 Joseph Mary Plunkett, in *Prose and Poetry of England,* ed. by H. Ward McCraw, Chicago, The Singer Company, 1934

49 *Orthodoxy and the Ecological Crisis*, 1999

50 Killian McDonnell, 'The Baptism of Jesus in the Jordon', Collegeville, Minnesota, Liturgical Press, 1996, p. 243

51 ibid ., p. 244

52 George Monbiot, 'Beware of the appliance of Science', *Guardian*, 24 February 2000, p. 22

53 Eilis Ryan, 'Saving the Earth', *Farmers Journal*, 15 May 1999, p. 3

54 Bishop Bill Murphy, 'Going to the Father's House. A Jubilee People', Pastoral Letter to the Diocese of Kerry, 1999

extensive building in the late 1850's. These never came to fruition and only two model houses were ever built. In the early part of the 20th century houses were built on the Mouth Charles Estate and 22 at McSweeney Terrace. Later in the 1970s, 78 houses were built in the Marian Estate. These houses are occupied all year round.

During the 1990s the face of Kilkee was transformed and deformed by a feverish building programme which was driven by tax inducements. I will argue here that the planning contravened three fundamental principles of planning namely, that it should be *ecologically sustainable, socially just and architecturally appropriate.*

Housing Boom

The number of houses in Kilkee prior to 1990 was 595, of which 428 were occupied all year round. This means that 71.9% of the housing stock was inhabited throughtout the year at that time. From 1992 to 1998 a total of 643 new houses were built in Kilkee. This is an increase of 132.77 per cent in the number of houses. Interestingly enough, the dramatic increase in housing has not lead to a massive increase in the permanent population. Of the 643 houses built, only 38 were built for permanent residents. Most of the houses that have been built are holiday houses and so are only occupied for a few months of the year. Those who occupy them then have very little permanent engagement with the community. At the moment only 34.25% of housing in Kilkee is inhabited all year round.

Inadequate sewage and water facilities

In contravention of any rational planning process the building spree took place with woefully inadequate sewage and water facilities. Even in 2001 Kilkee is still dependent on the sewage system that was upgraded in 1974. Untreated sewage is discharged into the ocean west of the town in Intrinsic Bay.

There is no definite plan to upgrade the present sewage system to meet the 2005 EU directive, which demands that untreated sewage should not be discharged into the ocean. In a letter dated 12 September 2000 the County Engineer, Mr T. Carey, stated that 'In the Council's Assessment of Needs of February 2000 the provision of sewage treatment in Kilkee was prioritised at No. 5. Unfortunately, Kilkee did not feature in the recently announced Water Service Investment Programme.'

The water system is also inadequate. During the summer months many residents of the Miltown Road and McSweeney Tce cannot take a shower until after midnight due to insufficient water pressure. In some households filling a kettle is quite tedious as the water comes in just a trickle. One household has bought four washing machines in a period of four years.

Houses have been built on almost every available scrap of land in the town. There is no provision for a public park, for sporting where some young person can kick a ball or puck a *sliotar* or play basketball during the long winter evenings.

St Joseph's Community College, the only secondary school in the peninsula, has a population of 335 students. The school has no gym, no hall, no track or playing pitch. If it were not for the local GAA, who have a pitch outside the town, there would be no facilities for young people at all. One does not need to be a social worker to realise that the lack of adequate playing and recreation facilities can contribute to young people experimenting with drugs and alcohol. The planning process seems to overlook these basic needs.

The influence of the building programme on the local economy is very significant. In 1998 a holiday home on the Miltown Road cost £140,000. A small number of houses in the Moore Bay complex were advertised for local purchase at £78,000. How can a local young couple buy a house at such inflationary prices? I do not know of any effective scheme either at the local, county or national level which is actually addressing this kind of imbalance which, in large part, was created by government sponsored tax breaks for the well-off.

I feel that one could justifiably make the point that it is socially unjust to favour well-off people who do not live in the community, and who contribute very little to its well-being, with tax breaks to build holiday houses that will be empty for the best part of the year at a time when the pressing need for social housing is being starved of public resources.

Just looking at what has happened it would seem that the planning authorities and the builders had only one idea in mind. Build as many houses as possible in every available piece of land. Some houses that had a view of the ocean in the mid-90s had this view completely obstructed by the next phase of the building programme. The only view from one house now is up into the sky.

Given the record of the past few years my fear is that since every free spot in town has been built upon, the planners will sanction a building programme for the most exclusive clients on the coast road leading out to the Golleen. This is a sensitive habitat for choughs. They need lands that are grazed and closely cropped by cattle. If the present habitat is destroyed and replaced by houses with lawns in front of them this will mean the end of the chough population. But will that deter planners from sanctioning ribbon development along the road? If the last ten years are anything to go by the answer must be an emphatic no.

Beach

Kilkee, with its large circular beach of firm sand and lack of currents is an ideal spot for swimming, especially for young children. It is important for its tourist reputation that a seaside resort like Kilkee retains its prestigious Blue Flag status. The Blue Flag scheme is an initiative of the Foundation for Environmental Education in Europe (a network of 22 non-government organisations). In Ireland the scheme is administered by An Taisce with financial support from the Department of the Environment. To receive the Blue Flag the beach must meet the criteria laid down in the EU Directive on Quality of Bathing Waters and the Local Authority must ensure that adequate sanitary services and infrastructure are in place. The Local Authority must sample the water every two weeks during the bathing season for faecal bacteria and other pollutants.

Kilkee had a Blue Flag until 1995. It lost it between 1996 and 1998. The reason seemed to be that at least one of the two streams flowing across the beach – the Victoria Stream or the Atlantic Stream – was polluted. In the Summer of 1998 Clare County Council erected a sign stating that 'This stream and the immediate vicinity is at present unsuitable for bathing or paddling due to recent high levels of bacteria. Please swim in approved designated area as indicated by buoys and signage.' A hundred yards along the beach another sign read: 'Bathing Permitted'. At a public meeting called by the Planning Review Group in August 1998 the local GP told a packed hall that Clare County Council were obviously dealing with a very intelligent bacteria that would avoid floating where the sign said no bathing.

In 1999 and again in 2000 I noticed that the mouth of the Victoria Stream was blocked up when I visited in June, July and August. Once in 1999, after a flood, the waters burst through the dam. The structure in 2000 seemed more sophisticated with something verging on a sluice mechanism. In September 1999 and again in September 2000, the 12th to be exact, the 'dam' was removed and the stream was allowed to flow freely through the strand out to the sea. My question is: what is the purpose of this 'dam'? Is it a way of dealing with the fact that the Victoria Stream is polluted? Is it about retaining the Blue Flag? On 19 September I wrote to the Deputy County Manager, Mr Tom Carey, raising these questions. If any of these suggestions are correct, the Council